A Vampire is NOT a Pet

Lexi Rees

OUTSET

Published in Great Britain

By Outset Publishing Ltd

First edition published September 2025

Written by Lexi Rees

Cover design by Miraworth Designs

ISBN: 978-1-913799-21-2

www.lexirees.co.uk

Chapter 1

The Advertisement

Forget cats! Forget dogs!

This Christmas, why not adopt a unique creature that never needs walks, hardly eats a thing, and sleeps all day? Ideal for busy families.

The picture underneath the advert was so blurry it could have been a hedgehog. Or a hamster. Or possibly a burnt sausage with eyes.

'Darling!' Mum shoved the phone under Dad's nose, crumpling his newspaper. 'I've found the perfect present for Yasmin. She's been begging for a pet.'

Dad grunted. 'Mmm. As long as it doesn't shed hair on my slippers or need walking at six in the morning, fine by me.'

Mum squinted at the screen and scrolled down to read the details.

Looking for a Unique and Exciting Christmas Gift?
Sink Your Teeth into Our New Collection of Low Maintenance Creatures!

Are you tired of the same boring old pets? Want something unique to show off to your friends and family? We have the perfect solution for you!

All our creatures have simple dietary requirements, making them easy to care for.

And the best part? Since they sleep all day, there's no need to walk them while the children are at school. Ideal for busy families.

Limited-time special bonus offer: Order now and receive a set of free fake vampire teeth. Just imagine the hilarious photo opportunities with your new friend! Hurry, this fang-tastic offer won't last long!

Delivery in time for Christmas for orders placed in the next thirteen minutes.

www.draculand.com

Warning: We supply an instruction manual with each creature. Please study this carefully. Like any creature, they may bite when surprised, frightened, or hungry. Please use caution when handling and be sure to keep it away from objects that may be harmful. This store is not responsible for any mishaps that may occur.

There was some small print below that which said, "*Terms and conditions: No refunds, exchange programme optional.*" But nobody reads the small print. Mum put her phone down. 'Apparently, it eats almost nothing and sleeps all day, so we won't even need to find someone to look after it while she's at school and we're at work.'

'Fine by me,' Dad repeated.

'It says I need to order now to get delivery in time for Christmas. It'll be a lovely surprise.'

'Order it then. By the way, have you seen the time? You're late for work.'

Mum dug her credit card out of her bag and quickly typed in the details before grabbing her coat and sprinting out the door. On the bus, she thought about the order. As long as it wasn't a snake, or worse, a tarantula, it would be fine. And the blurry picture had definitely looked more like a small rodent than a snake or spider.

She searched through her Facebook feed but couldn't find the ad. She checked her email, but there was no confirmation of the order. She scratched her head. 'What was the website?' she muttered. 'Drakeland?' Was it a kind of duck? 'Dragonland?' Was it even legal to sell dragons? She did a quick online search for drakeland.com and dragonland.com, but nothing came up. With a sinking feeling, she decided it was a scam. 'I'd better call the bank and cancel my credit card,' she said with a sigh as she got off the bus outside the office, mentally adding it to the bottom of the already far too long to-do list. And as the busy working day started, that is exactly where it stayed.

Chapter 2

The Fang-tastic Present

It was 3.13 a.m. on Christmas Day and all through the house, not a creature was stirring, not even a mouse... well, except for Yasmin. She was as still as a kangaroo on a pogo stick, jumping up and down on her bed as she waited for Santa to arrive.

Suddenly, a loud KNOCK echoed through the silent house, making Yasmin jump even higher. Everybody knew Santa came down the chimney. He definitely didn't knock at the front door. So, who could it be? Excitedly, she tiptoed to the window and squinted into the night. She couldn't see anything.

KNOCK! KNOCK! The noise was louder this time.

Pulling on her fluffy pink dressing gown and matching slippers, Yasmin sprinted down the stairs like a hyperactive flamingo. She wasn't tall enough to see through the spyhole, so she peeped through the letterbox. Nobody. She cracked open the door and peeked outside.

On the porch lay an odd-looking, diamond-shaped wooden box. It was almost as big as she was and had the words '*Handle with Care*' painted on the side in big red letters, a large stamp which read www.draculand.com, and a sticker that proclaimed, '*This way up* >'. The box was *not* that way up. With a mighty heave, Yasmin flipped the box over per the instructions, because it is very important to follow instructions properly, and dragged it inside.

From inside the box, a faint scratching sound echoed. The more she jostled the box, the louder the scratching grew. Yasmin dashed to the kitchen, grabbed a pair of scissors, and began a battle with the stubborn sticky tape. Finally, the lid popped open a few inches, and a musty smell filled the air. It reminded her of Grandpa's old socks.

She peered inside and saw... a tiny bat. Apart from the bat and some red velvet fabric, it was completely empty. Now, some people might find a bat a bit scary, but not Yasmin. Her first thought was it was furry, cute, and purring like a kitten. And her second thought was, can you have a bat as a pet? Her friends had dogs and cats, but a bat? Nobody had a bat. This was bat-tastic!

Just then, Mum stumbled down the stairs, rubbing the sleep from her eyes. 'What's all the racket?'

Yasmin flung her arms around her and gave her a big bear hug. 'Thank you for the best Christmas present ever. I know you were worried that I wasn't responsible enough for a dog or cat. I won't let you down, I promise.'

Mum looked at the presents under the tree, still wrapped, puzzled. Yasmin, too excited for words, pointed at the box. Mum squinted at the website address printed on the box and gasped.

'Oh my goodness. It arrived. I thought that was a scam.'

She lifted the lid and looked inside the box. But she didn't see a small bat. What she saw was a perfectly normal-sized girl with a very pale face. The girl's eyes pinged open, shining a bright ruby red. Mum sprung back as if she'd had an electric shock.

The girl pushed the lid the rest of the way off the box and sat up, flashing a grin and revealing a pair of fangs that would put a sabre-toothed tiger to shame.

'Hello. I'm Velma, the vampire you ordered.'

'The w-what?' Mum stammered, eyeing the vampire like a ticking time bomb. Suddenly the prospect of a snake, tarantula, or even a dragon seemed appealing. 'Is it safe to have a vampire in the house? What's the refund policy?'

'Sorry, no refunds, just the exchange programme,' Velma said cheerfully. 'But don't worry, I come with full instructions. Like how to avoid getting your neck bitten...' She giggled. 'Just kidding! I don't bite. Often.'

With that, Mum fainted.

Velma tilted her head to the side, curious. 'Oops. Did I scare her? I promise I'm not dangerous.'

Yasmin took a deep breath. True, she had longed for a pet, preferably something cute and cuddly, and a bat was perhaps pushing it a little, but a pet vampire... well, that was a completely different kettle of fish.

As if reading her thoughts, Velma spoke up. 'I know I'm probably not quite what you were expecting – I've already told the marketing department their advert is a bit iffy – but I promise we'll have the most fun ever.'

'Oh dear,' Mum mumbled, pushing herself upright. 'A vampire. Your definition of "fun" is exactly what I'm worried about.'

Velma chuckled. 'Don't worry, I'm good as gold. I had the most house points at vampire school last year, even more than Luna, which everyone thought was impossible. Nice necklace, by the way, although I prefer silver. Did you know it's a complete myth that vampires can't touch silver? Look.' Velma waved her arm, displaying a silver charm bracelet. She pointed at a silver tooth dangling from it. 'I got this from the Fang Fairy when I lost my first fang. And this bat charm was to celebrate my first successful transformation. And this silver feather was for my first flight, although I did crash into a tree and there was some debate about whether I deserved it, but that was just Viktor being mean. And this one—'

'We get it,' Yasmin's mum interrupted.

Velma lowered her arm and looked Mum straight

in the eye. 'I promise I won't bite you. Please don't send me back. I'll be a laughingstock at school if I get sent home so early. Here, I was told to give you this as soon as I arrived.' Velma held out a leaflet. 'I know humans always read instruction manuals carefully.'

Chapter 3

The Rules

Mum seemed to be frozen to the spot, so Yasmin took the leaflet. On the front cover, it read, *Your Howl-to Guide to Vampire Care.* She opened it, squinted at the fancy blood-red print, and read aloud.

Instructions for the proper care and maintenance of your vampire.

1. Your vampire's tummy rumbles are not to be ignored. Feed it as soon as the moon is up to avoid any 'oopsies' during the night.
2. Saying 'stake' around your vampire is like telling a cat you're out of tuna. They might take it as a threat and get defensive. Same goes for 'steak'. It can cause serious

confusion. To avoid any potentially fatal mix-ups around dinner time, consider turning the whole household vegetarian.

3. Keep your vampire away from giraffes. Too much neck. Way too tempting.
4. Do not leave your vampire alone with any garlic. Allergic reactions vary, but common symptoms include hiccups and making them more irritable than a teenager without Wi-Fi. Prepare for sulks and eye-rolls.
5. Avoid perfume. You'd be surprised how many perfumes can turn into eau de garlic on a hot day.
6. If your vampire sparkles in the sun, don't panic. Reach out to your nearest *Twilight** fan club – they've got advice on this.
7. Remember, your vampire is *not* a pet rock. Please do not paint their nails or put them in a tutu (unless they ask, of course!).

*Ask a grown-up about the *Twilight* movies/books. The fan club has free training for all your vampire co-living needs.

. . .

If I can follow these rules, then I'll show everyone I can handle this. Velma will be happy, and we'll all be safe, Yasmin thought, folding the leaflet and tucking it into her pocket. 'Doesn't sound too hard, does it, Mum? Please can we keep her? I promise I'll look after Velma all by myself.'

Still pale from the shock, Mum gave a hesitant look. 'A vampire as a pet? I'm not sure that's a good idea.'

A fat tear slid down Yasmin's cheek.

Mum handed her a tissue. 'Look, we'll chat about this with your dad tomorrow morning. For now, let's find a... safe spot for her?'

Before Yasmin could answer, Velma chimed in. 'No worries, ladies. That economy coffin ride from Transylvania was worse than forgetting your sunscreen. Can you believe they stacked me upside down? I need to catch up on my beauty sleep.' With that, she lay down in her coffin and shut the lid.

Mum stared at the box for a few minutes, shrugged, and went upstairs.

Yasmin followed her mum upstairs, but once snuggled in her own bed, she couldn't sleep. She tossed and turned, her mind racing with thoughts of the new pet. She tried counting sheep, but they kept turning into bats and flying away, so she gave up.

With a sigh, she got up and went over to her desk. She pulled out a notebook and a sparkly pink pen, and brainstormed a list of reasons they should keep Velma:

1. Imagine the look on everyone's faces at school show-and-tell.
2. I'll become an expert in dental hygiene.
3. Halloween costume? Sorted.
4. Say goodbye to mosquito bites.

Yasmin hesitated. Would Velma as a bat eat mosquitoes, or were they rivals in their blood-sucking abilities? She put a line through the last reason. It wasn't a very good list, but it was a start.

Next morning, armed with her list and the determination to prove to Mum and Dad that she was responsible enough to look after a pet, Yasmin went down for breakfast. After a long debate, they agreed to let her keep Velma.

'On a trial basis,' Dad said. Three times.

'We're trusting you. Remember, last time you promised to water that pot plant, it ended up like burnt toast,' Mum added.

In celebration, Yasmin stood up and closed the kitchen blinds.

Dad blinked. 'Why are you shutting out the sun? It's a beautiful day.'

‘Because...’ Yasmin said, grinning, ‘I’m going to wake up Velma and tell her she can stay.’

Mum quickly pulled up her shirt collar and tossed Yasmin a scarf. ‘Better put this on first. We don’t want Velma confusing your neck with a juice box.’

Chapter 4

The Garlic Bread Incident

Yasmin was buzzing with excitement to show off her new pet. What better way to introduce Velma to her friends than by having a pizza party, she'd thought. Because nothing says 'Welcome to the gang' quite like an extra cheesy slice of pizza, right?

When the doorbell chimed on Friday afternoon, Yasmin sprinted to the door. Her friends stood on the porch, each carrying various snacks.

Sophie held a plate of garlic bread, wafting a warm, mouth-watering scent into the air. Yasmin placed the garlic bread next to the pizzas, and everyone descended on the food like a pack of ravenous werewolves.

Suddenly, Velma's ruby-red eyes lit up like fireworks, and she licked her fangs. Yasmin felt a twinge of unease. She suspected something was wrong, but she couldn't put her finger on it.

Just as Velma stretched a hand towards the garlic bread, it hit Yasmin. 'Wait, don't eat the–!'

But it was too late. Velma had already taken a great big bite, and the garlicky butter was trickling down her chin. Trying to grab the rest of the slice, Yasmin lunged at her, but Velma was far too quick and darted across the room like a hyperactive squirrel.

'Velma! Stop! Don't eat it! You're allergic to garlic!' Yasmin cried out, remembering the instructions, but Velma had never tasted anything so delicious in her entire undead life and was far too busy gorging on her newfound favourite food to listen.

She dodged Yasmin's grasp with ease and darted around the room, all the time with a chunk of garlic bread clasped in her hand, cramming it into her mouth like it was her last meal. And this is how the great garlic bread chase began.

Velma scrambled over the sofa, dived under the dining table, clambered over a chair, and ducked behind the TV, round and round, never missing an opportunity to swipe another slice of the forbidden garlic bread on her way past. The living room became a battlefield, and Velma, armed with her prized possession (yet another slice of garlic bread), was winning.

Velma only stopped when she finished the garlic bread. The children collapsed on the sofa, their faces red and sweaty from the chase.

'Eww. What's that pong?' Otto asked, holding his nose.

Sophie sniffed the air. 'I think it's coming from Velma,' she said, pointing to the vampire.

Velma let out a loud belch, and a cloud of garlic breath wafted across the room, causing everyone to cover their noses.

'Who knew vampires could be so stinky?' Sophie

added as the putrid waft of garlic breath filled the room. She sprayed some air freshener and lit a lavender-scented candle, but it only made the smell worse.

Yasmin and her friends held their noses as the smell grew stronger and stronger. They flung open the windows, but Velma's garlic breath was so potent that pedestrians on the street outside swerved to avoid the stench.

Sophie rummaged through her bag, searching for a packet of minty-fresh chewing gum. 'What about this?' she asked, holding up the pack.

'Good idea,' Yasmin said.

Velma took the gum, but before anybody could tell her you're supposed to chew it, she swallowed the packet whole. 'Hic,' she said with a loud hiccup.

Yasmin groaned. 'Oh no. Now she has hiccups *and* stinky breath.'

'Hic,' Velma hiccuped in agreement.

'Hold your breath,' Chiyo suggested.

Velma rolled her eyes. 'I'm the undead. I don't breathe.'

Yasmin clapped her hands. 'I know how to cure hiccups. We have to scare them out of you.'

Sophie nodded enthusiastically. 'Prepare to be terrified, Velma. Close your eyes while we get ready.'

Otto hid behind the door, ready to jump out with a roar. Sophie grabbed a bedsheet from the laundry closet, intending to transform into a ghost, and Yasmin practised pulling the scariest faces she could make.

'On three,' Yasmin whispered. 'One... two... three.'

Otto bumped his head on the door frame mid leap and his roar turned into a wail. Sophie tripped over the hem of the sheet, landing on the floor in a tangled mess. And Yasmin's attempts at scary faces were just plain silly. Velma burst into laughter and hiccuped again. The scare plan had flopped.

'Try drinking some water upside down,' Yasmin suggested, rushing to get a glass. Velma drank it standing on her head, hardly spilling a drop. Yet, as she stood up, 'Hic,' she went again.

'Tickle attack,' declared Otto, launching himself at Velma with wiggling fingers. Velma squirmed and laughed, momentarily forgetting the hiccups, but as soon as the tickling stopped, 'Hic,' there it was again, as stubborn as ever.

'What if we just ignore them?' Sophie asked.

So, they switched the TV on and pretended to watch a cookery show. Finally, as if by magic (or perhaps just the passage of time), Velma's hiccups subsided.

'See? They're gone. It worked,' Yasmin said

triumphantly, even though she was unsure which of their attempts had actually been the remedy.

Velma smiled, happy to be hiccup-free. 'Maybe it was the scare after all. It's not often someone tries to scare a vampire.' Then she burped.

'Aargh,' Otto, who was sitting next to her, screamed. 'We may have scared away your hiccups, but it didn't solve your stinky breath.'

Chiyo leapt up and ran to the herb garden, reappearing with a handful of fresh parsley. She held it out to Velma. 'Eat it. My granny says it helps with bad breath.'

'Green. Yucky,' Velma said, clamping her fangs shut and refusing to even taste it.

Holly passed Velma a lemon. Velma's fangs pierced the skin and released a jet of juice, which shot straight into her eye. Velma had never tasted anything so sour in her entire undead life. She jumped up and down, clutching her eye with one hand while covering her mouth with the other.

Velma gargled with milk. She rubbed a raw onion on her tongue. As a last resort, she even tried brushing her teeth. But nothing worked. They were doomed to suffer the consequences of the garlic mishap.

The friends slumped back onto the sofa again. Velma burped again, so loudly the lampshade shook.

Holly squeaked. Chiyo fanned herself. Sophie groaned. 'Too... much... garlic...' Otto moaned before dashing for the door shouting, 'Fresh air! FRESH AIR!'

With a chorus of hurried goodbyes and promises to meet again (preferably in a garlic-free zone), Yasmin's friends were gone and the living room was silent again. Silent except for Velma, who sat in the middle of the sofa, crumbs all over her lap, cheerfully licking garlic butter off her fingers between burps.

Yasmin sighed. 'Well...' she said, surveying the wreckage of crisp packets, juice cartons, and one mysteriously abandoned sock, 'I guess it's just you, me, and your radioactive burps now.'

Velma's shoulders sagged. 'Sorry. I didn't mean to spoil your party. I always ruin everything. You'd be better off without me.'

'Don't be silly, I know you didn't mean it. But like hamsters can't eat avocado, maybe next time you could avoid the garlic bread?'

'Did you just compare me to a hamster? I'm not a pet,' Velma huffed, transforming into a bat. With an angry squeak (can bats burp?), she flew out of the window.

Yasmin stood at the window, arms crossed, bits of garlic bread still stuck in her hair. 'Brilliant,' she muttered. 'I've just been told off by a bat.' She plopped down on the sofa, clutching a cushion to her chest. Her eyes flicked to the crumbs scattered across the carpet and the half-empty breadbasket on the table. 'If garlic can wreck a party that badly,' she sighed, 'I'm going to need an instruction manual the size of a mountain.'

Chapter 5

The Blood Bank Heist

The first rays of sunlight poked their nosy noses through the window. Mum stuck her head through the door to Yasmin's bedroom.

'Wakey, wakey. First day of the school holidays,' she said, her eyes twinkling like disco balls. 'We're going camping!'

After breakfast, the family flew around the house like busy bees, grabbing blankets, clothes and kitchen items, as well as camping and fishing equipment.

'Where are the tents?' Mum bellowed from the basement.

'Where are my hiking boots?' Dad hollered from the hall.

'You're wearing them,' Yasmin pointed out. Dad turned as red as a beetroot.

Yasmin took charge of packing Velma's things,

including a cooler bag with Velma's Plasma-Power food pellets.

Finally, they'd squashed everything into the car and piled in. Yasmin scrunched up between two tents, with a suitcase jammed under her feet, which pushed her knees up to her chin like a human pretzel. Velma curled into a ball, pulled a blanket over her head, and went to sleep.

After setting up the tents, they went for a long walk in the woods, then cooked dinner over the campfire, eating gooey toasted marshmallows on sticks until they felt sick. Then they snuggled into their sleeping bags for the night. The camp fell silent. An owl hooted, waking Velma up. She nudged Yasmin.

'All this fresh air is making me hungry,' she said, her stomach growling.

'I'll get your breakfast,' Yasmin said, unzipping her sleeping bag and crawling out, but there was no sign of the cooler bag. She remembered packing the food. And she remembered putting it on the kitchen counter. But she didn't remember loading it into the car. 'Velma, I've left your special food at home. Now Mum and Dad will think I'm not responsible enough to look after a pet.'

'Not a pet,' Velma muttered under her breath. 'But I am hungry,' she said louder, her stomach grumbling again to reinforce the message. 'I wish I could eat normal food like your friends. I don't want to be the weird kid all the time.'

Yasmin's eyes narrowed in determination. She was not going to let Velma, or her parents, down. Looking after a pet was harder than she had expected, but she was going to fix this all by herself. 'Don't worry, Velma. We can go to the shop. We passed one on the way here that said it was open twenty-four hours a day.'

The road they had driven down was long and windy. 'I'm going to use my BatNav to find a shortcut,' Velma said. With a wink, she started to shrink. She wiggled her toes, and they curled into cute bat claws. Leathery bat wings sprung from her shoulder blades and, after a bit of frantic flapping, she did a loop-de-loop, nearly crashed into one of the guy ropes, and landed on Yasmin's head. 'Ta-da! BatNav mode engaged! Next stop, breakfast.'

At first, everything seemed fine. Velma flitted ahead, her bat wings fluttering softly in the cool night air. Yasmin jogged behind, struggling to keep up as Velma darted about. But as they delved deeper into the woods, Velma hovered in mid-air, her tiny bat brows furrowed in concentration as if trying to read invisible street signs, and Yasmin wondered if they were lost. Finally, they came to a halt at a familiar-looking duck pond.

Yasmin frowned. 'Uh, Velma, we've been here before. I think the BatNav is taking us in circles.'

'Absolutely not. It's just... uh, calculating the shortest route.'

Yasmin shrugged and started jogging, but before they knew it, they found themselves back at the pond. This time the ducks quacked, angry at having their sleep disturbed yet again.

'Oopsie-daisy,' Velma said, hanging upside down from a tree branch, looking sheepish. 'I think my BatNav took us on a wild-goose chase, or should I say, a wild-duck chase.' And so, with the BatNav declared officially 'quackers', Velma returned to her vampire form.

Yasmin decided to continue their adventure the old-fashioned way, by following the footpath. This took them straight up the main road to a cluster of buildings. As they approached the grocery store, Yasmin's heart sank at the sight of a piece of paper taped to the door with large letters spelling out 'CLOSED'.

'I thought you said this was open all night,' Velma grumbled.

'It should be,' Yasmin said, pointing to a flashing neon sign in the window proclaiming: OPEN ALL HOURS. 'I guess business is a bit slack at this time of night, so I can't say I blame them. What do we do now?'

Velma's red eyes glinted. 'I have a plan so brilliant, it needs sunglasses. There's a doctor's surgery over there, on the other side of the park. We're going to the blood bank.'

Yasmin's eyes widened. 'A *blood bank*? You mean a bank?'

'Sort of. Only instead of money, it's full of blood. People go there to make withdrawals, but instead of cash, they get a pint of the lifesaving stuff. And we're in luck, because there's one just over there.' She pointed across the park.

As they approached it, Yasmin's heart sank. There was no kiosk; the building was locked up tighter than a jar of pickles.

'What do we do?' Yasmin asked.

'There's only one thing we can do – we're going to break in,' Velma declared. 'We'll be like bank robbers. Think of it as opening a savings account. Only I'm saving myself from starving.'

Suddenly, Yasmin grabbed her arm and dragged her behind a tree. 'Wait!' She pointed towards the clinic where the silhouette of a tall, thin figure wearing a long black cloak slunk through the shadows towards the front door.

With Yasmin holding her breath (and Velma unbreathing as usual), they watched the sinister figure produce a small leather case from deep within the folds of the cloak. With nimble fingers, the figure flicked it open, revealing a shiny silver toolkit, glinting in the pale moonlight. Yasmin and Velma watched in awe as the figure picked the lock. A second later, the door clicked open, and the figure slipped inside.

'Whoa, who was that?' Velma whispered.

'I don't know, looks like a burglar. And they just made picking a lock look easier than using a key. Let's see what they're up to.'

They crept closer to the blood bank clinic; their footsteps were barely audible against the soft grass beneath their feet. As they approached, they noticed the door was slightly ajar. Velma giggled. 'They might be good at opening doors, but they're not so good at closing them.' She reached out, pushed it open, stepped inside, and crashed straight into the burglar. With a yelp, he tumbled backward, landing in a heap.

Rubbing his head, the burglar sat up. Then he froze as his dark eyes landed on the two girls. 'What are you two doing here?' he demanded.

Yasmin's mind raced as she tried to think of an excuse. She glanced at Velma, hoping for inspiration, but the vampire looked as panicked as she was.

'We, uh, we were looking for the bathroom,' Yasmin stammered, her voice squeakier than a rusty hinge.

The burglar looked sceptical. 'I don't think so,' he snarled. 'I'll give you one more chance to tell me what you're doing here.'

Knowing she had no choice, Yasmin decided honesty was the best policy. 'It's for my friend. I forgot to pack her special food.'

The burglar raised an eyebrow. 'Is that so?'

Yasmin swallowed hard. 'Yes. She's a vampire. And she's very hungry.'

To reinforce the point, Velma grinned, her fangs gleaming.

The burglar's scowl turned into a smile as he

beamed back at Velma, revealing a matching set of fangs. 'Well, why didn't you say so?' he asked. He rummaged in his loot bag and picked out several packets of plasma pellets, tossing them over. 'Always happy to help a fellow creature of the night. These are the best flavour. Almost as good as chocolate, with a hint of salted caramel. Now scoot,' he said, shooing them out of the door like they were naughty kids caught with their hands in a cookie jar.

They scarpered, following the path back to the campsite rather than attempting to use the BatNav again.

Safely back at the tent and tucked up in her sleeping bag, Yasmin looked at the pile of pellets. 'At least we got them, but I'll definitely pack more carefully next time.'

Chapter 6

The Flossing Fiasco

Yasmin strolled into the living room, only to find Velma sprawled across the couch, moaning and clutching her face. 'What's wrong, Velma?' she asked, concerned.

'It hurts,' Velma whined. 'I've got fang-ache. If I wasn't already dead, it would be killing me.'

'All right, Drac, time to do a little fang cleaning,' Yasmin said, brandishing a piece of dental floss.

Velma dived behind the couch. 'No way. It hurts too much.'

Yasmin scratched her head, wondering how to make the idea of flossing less scary. She had an idea. 'Why do vampires keep their fangs squeaky clean?'

Velma squinted suspiciously at Yasmin.

'To prevent bat breath,' Yasmin cackled, but Velma just blinked.

Velma's eyes widened. 'What's wrong with bat breath?'

'I don't know. What does bat breath smell like?'

'Garlicky.'

Yasmin rolled her eyes. 'Well, I'm afraid you still need to floss. What do you call the fear of flossing your teeth?'

Velma sighed. 'Is this another bad joke?'

Yasmin ignored her and delivered the punchline: 'Flosstrophobia!'

Velma shook her head. 'That's not even funny. And I'm still not going to floss.'

'In that case, if you won't floss, we're going to have to go to the dentist. Oh, I've thought of another dentist joke. Why did the vampire go to the dentist?'

Velma shook her head. 'I'm almost afraid to ask.'

'To improve his bite.'

Velma let out a long sigh. 'Are you going to keep on torturing me with these jokes until I agree to go to the dentist?'

'Definitely.'

'But what if the dentist finds out something's wrong with my fangs? I can't be a vampire without my fangs.'

'Then they'll fix it. That's their job. Do you want me to tell you another dentist joke?'

Velma sighed. 'Anything is better than your jokes. I'll book an appointment.'

On arrival at the dental clinic, they went straight to the reception desk. 'We've got an appointment,' Yasmin said, and Velma gave the receptionist her biggest smile.

The receptionist paled. 'What time is it b-booked for?'

'Tooth hurty,' Yasmin replied.

The receptionist stared at her blankly.

'Two thirty. Get it?' Yasmin said.

The receptionist shook his head. He was already having a bad day and was not in the mood for dentist jokes. Or any jokes come to think of it. 'Wait over there,' he said, pointing towards two lumpy armchairs in the corner of the room. 'Watch for your name coming up on that screen.'

After what seemed like an eternity, the screen flashed up a message: *Velma to Room 4*.

Yasmin dragged Velma towards Room 4 and pushed her into the dentist's chair.

The dentist turned around, took one look at Velma's fangs, and did what any sensible dentist would do – he ran out of the room screaming.

'What do we do now?' Velma asked.

'I'm sure he'll be back. It's probably just his first

time seeing a vampire,' Yasmin said, trying to sound reassuring.

After a few minutes, the dentist tiptoed back in, glancing nervously at Velma. 'Are you sure this is safe?' he asked.

Yasmin nodded confidently. 'She's a vampire, but don't worry, she won't bite.'

The dentist relaxed a bit. 'Ah, so her bark is worse than her bite?'

Velma looked puzzled. 'Bark? That's werewolves. I don't bark.'

'It was a joke,' the dentist said, getting the tools ready. 'Open wide... wow, those fangs are impressive.'

'Really?' Velma said. 'They are a bit smaller than the best vampires have.'

'Well, I think they are quite splendid,' the dentist said. He tried to check Velma's teeth with a mirror on a stick, but vampires don't have a reflection so he couldn't see anything. 'Hmm, this is tricky. They didn't teach vampire dentistry at school. I'll have to improvise,' he said, prodding Velma's teeth with a dental tool. But the moment it touched Velma's sore fang, the metal tool snapped like a twig.

He tried a bigger one, and it suffered the same fate. Velma's fangs were tougher than tungsten.

'I think this is a job for a different tooth fairy,' the dentist said, discarding the broken instruments. 'Luckily, I know just the person.'

'Who?' Yasmin asked, curious.

'The vet from the zoo. They deal with sabre-toothed tigers. They'll know how to handle vampire fangs.'

The dentist whipped out his phone and made a quick call. 'She'll be here in ten minutes. Wait here.'

Nine and a half minutes later, the dentist reappeared followed by the vet. 'Good afternoon, I believe we have a fang-tastic emergency?'

'Yes,' Velma said, opening her mouth wide.

The vet looked inside and nodded. 'Impressive fangs. Most vampires neglect their dental hygiene, but it seems like someone has been taking good care of these chompers.'

Velma blushed, showing off her fangs. 'I do like to keep my fangs in tip-top condition.'

'I can tell. But this fang here has a chip. That's why you've got fang-ache. I need to file it down.'

Velma winced. 'Will it hurt?'

'Not at all. I'm a professional. You'd be surprised how many vampire teeth I've been called upon to fix over the years. I've been everywhere from Transylvania to Timbuktu. Now hold still.' The vet got to work, carefully filing down Velma's chipped fang. 'I remember the first vampire I ever treated. He was from Transylvania, of course. And very very old. His teeth were so long, he could barely close his mouth. Now, that's all done. Would you like a quick polish to finish?'

'Yeth pleeth, 'Velma said, her mouth full of tools.

Once he was done, the vet pressed a button and Velma's chair rose into an upright position.

'That wasn't so bad, was it, Velma?' Yasmin said.

Velma smiled, flashing her newly polished fangs.

As they were leaving, Velma stopped and turned to the vet. 'What did the vampire say after the dentist checked her teeth?'

The vet scratched his head, intrigued.

'Fang you very much!' Velma said, her laughter

echoing down the hallway as they left.

Chapter 7

The Mistaken Identity

Velma's nose wrinkled as she sniffed at the bowl of crimson-red Plasma-Power food pellets. She let out a whimper and shuffled deeper under the blanket, as if trying to hide from the offending dish.

'What's wrong, Velma?' Yasmin asked. 'Don't you want your breakfast?'

Velma shook her head. She'd already tried to tempt Velma with a jar of Ghoulish Goulash, a can of Werewolf Whey, and even a packet of Banshee Biscuits, but Velma was having none of them.

Yasmin wracked her brain, trying to remember what the instruction manual Velma had arrived with said about feeding problems. She rummaged through her desk to find it, then flipped through the pages, scanning each one until she found the section on 'Problem solving'. She jabbed the page with her finger. 'I knew it was in here somewhere.'

When your beloved vampire companion is off their regular food, swift action is required to avoid potentially undesirable consequences. Some owners suggest offering them a nice bowl of chicken noodle soup or perhaps a raw steak. However, we highly recommend our special Haemoglobin Hors d'Oeuvres. This delectable blend of rare blood types will have your vampire feeling like royalty once again.

If your vampire is still hesitant to indulge in their special cuisine, try offering it in different forms. Some vampires prefer it raw, while others prefer it cooked. If all else fails, try hiding it in their favourite dish. You'd be surprised how much easier it is to get your vampire to eat their reds when it's mixed in with a bowl of spaghetti.

Remember, a happy vampire is a healthy vampire. So, stock up on Haemoglobin Hors d'Oeuvres today to keep your fanged friend in tiptop condition.

Yasmin vaguely remembered ordering a packet of *Haemoglobin Hors d'Oeuvres*. In the dim light of the pantry, she squinted at the labels, pushing aside cans and bottles and jars. She was about to give up when she spotted the small sachet at the back, hiding behind a stack of cans. She poured some into Velma's dish but Velma only sniffed at it suspiciously and turned away. Yasmin tried to coax her with encouraging words, but Velma still refused to eat.

Maybe she's just not hungry, Yasmin thought. *I'll leave it out for her to eat when she's ready.* Yasmin picked up her bag and hurried off to school. When she got home, she rushed upstairs to check on Velma. The bowl was empty, but Yasmin knew her friend wasn't well. Velma didn't want to play, and even the plasma popsicle Yasmin had picked up on the way home as a treat didn't cheer her up.

As the sun dipped below the horizon, Yasmin let her out into the garden where Velma knelt down and nibbled on a blade of grass.

Yasmin gasped. Velma NEVER ate her greens. Not even a tiny lettuce leaf. Not even under extreme bribery with plasma popsicles. She sprinted inside, skidding on the kitchen tiles, and yanked the empty sachet out of the recycling bin. Her eyes raced down the small print. 'May contain traces of... grass?' she muttered. That didn't sound right. She flipped the packet over—and her stomach dropped.

Bovine Buffet Blend.

Not Haemoglobin Hors d'Oeuvres.

'Oh no, no, no, no. I've turned my vampire into a vegetarian.'

From the garden came an unmistakable sound: *MOOOOO!*

Yasmin froze, her heart doing a somersault. She tiptoed to the back door and peeked outside.

Velma was standing in the flowerbed. Except... she wasn't exactly Velma anymore. She had 4 legs, her cloak had turned into a patchy black and white furry coat, her ears had gone floppy, and, between her sharp vampire fangs, a big, fat pink tongue lolled out.

'Maybe I'm not cut out to be a proper vampire.

Even my transformations go wrong,' Velma grumbled. Only it came out as; 'Moo moo moo MOOOO.'

Yasmin slapped her forehead. She was now the proud owner of the world's first vampire-cow. How was she going to fix this? She decided to take Velma for a long walk, hoping the exercise would get the food out of her system. As they reached the fields at the edge of town, Velma spotted a herd of cows and let out a loud 'moo'.

The farmer appeared from behind the hedge. 'There you are. I've been looking for you everywhere! You must be missing your mammy, poor little calf.'

'She's not your calf,' Yasmin explained, gently lifting Velma's lip to reveal her sharp fangs to show the farmer that she was, in fact, a vampire, despite appearances to the contrary.

The farmer scratched his head. 'Well, I'll be darned. I ain't never seen a calf with fangs before.'

Yasmin rolled her eyes. 'That's because she's not a calf. She's my pet vampire.'

'Not a pet,' Velma said, but of course all Yasmin and the farmer heard was, 'Moo'.

The farmer raised his eyebrows. 'A pet vampire that looks like a calf? I've heard it all now,' he said, chuckling to himself.

Yasmin smiled. 'Yes, exactly. And now we'd better

be going, she's not used to walking so far,' she said, nudging Velma along.

The farmer watched as Yasmin and Velma walked away. He shook his head in disbelief. 'If that's a pet vampire, I'll eat my hat,' he muttered to himself.

Velma the cow belched loudly.

'Better out than in,' Yasmin said.

Another burp, only this time, instead of 'Moo', it came out as; 'Actually... I think I'm feeling better now.' Velma's cow ears shrunk, her tail gave a final swish, and with a *pop!* she transformed back into her vampire self. 'Let's go home, I'm starving.'

Chapter 8

The Midnight Macarena

As the first rays of moonlight peeked through her bedroom curtains, the sound of crashing glass catapulted Yasmin out of her bed. She sprinted downstairs and into the kitchen. It looked like a tornado had hit it.

Velma was bouncing off the walls like a pinball on a sugar rush. Scattered across the floor, among the shattered remains of Mum's favourite vase, were the little red Plasma-Power food pellets. Velma had clearly fancied a midnight feast and the aftereffects were like a giant sugar-rush.

With an ear-splitting *CRASH*, Velma cannonballed through the window, leaving the room decorated in sparkly glass confetti.

Dad appeared at the kitchen door with a face like thunder.

'Sorry, Dad,' Yasmin said, grabbing her coat. 'I'll tidy this up later, but I need to catch Velma first.'

Outside, under the glow of the moon, Velma's eyes twinkled like disco balls as she dashed off in the distance.

'Stop, Velma!' Yasmin cried, chasing after her.

A breathless Yasmin finally arrived in the town square, just in time to see Velma clapping her hands above her head and tapping her feet like a flamenco dancer, encouraging a slightly bemused busker to pick up the beat. As music filled the plaza, people spilled out from the nearby bars and restaurants to join in the dance. Even a poodle wearing a frilly pink tutu joined in. Velma's spontaneous spooky salsa had turned into a full-blown vampire flash mob! She leapt into the air, landing in a whirling dervish, leading the dizzy dancers, and the poodle, on a wild midnight macarena like the Pied Piper of Hamelin.

In the commotion, nobody noticed a figure stumble from one of the grand houses that flanked the plaza. Mayor Goodwin, notorious for his impeccable suits and stern demeanour, was a spectacle that would make a peacock blush. His normally slicked-back hair jutted out in all directions, like a surprised porcupine and, instead of a smart office suit, he was wearing a pair of mismatched slippers and luminous polka-dotted pyjamas that were probably visible from outer space. As if that wasn't bad enough, a strange green goo was smeared all over his cheeks.

'Wha–what's all this ruckus?' he bumbled, squinting through his monocle. His eyes widened as they landed on the pirouetting poodle. 'Molly? Is that you?'

The poodle paused mid-twirl and yipped, making a beeline for the mayor and leaping into his arms. 'No, no, Molly, not the cucumber face mask!' he shrieked, but it was too late. The overexcited poodle licked off half of the green goo. The half of his face which was clean blushed bright red.

'Whoever started this frightful rumpus will be hearing from me first thing in the morning,' he shouted, before stomping back to his house and slamming the door behind him.

Yasmin caught Velma's elbow and whispered, 'I think now would be a good time for us to go home.'

Velma, with the sugar rush subsiding, stopped dancing and as suddenly as it had started, the party ended. Confusion engulfed the area like a heavy fog as the dancers looked around, trying to make sense of what had just happened, blissfully unaware of the power of a vampire mind over a crowd. Bit by bit, they returned to their tables, picking up their unfinished conversations over their plates of half-eaten dinners and lukewarm drinks.

Chapter 9

The Halloween Party

Halloween morning arrived with squeals, squeaks, and an alarming amount of glitter. Yasmin could barely sit still—this afternoon she was going to *the* party of the year. At three o'clock, she was so excited she practically ran all the way there, dragging Velma behind her like a kite on a string. In all the excitement, Yasmin completely forgot one *tiny* detail... to mention that everyone would be in fancy dress. So it took less than five seconds for Velma to spot another vampire.

'Oooh, he looks like my cousin Vlad,' she exclaimed, making her way over to the boy. 'Greetings, fellow nightwalker.'

Yasmin tugged at Velma's sleeve, hissing in her ear, 'It's just a costume.'

The boy's smile stretched wide, and a marvellous set of fake fangs jutted out from his lips. 'Indeed, tonight, I am a vampire.' He sniffed and then sneezed, causing the fangs to fly out of his mouth and into his glass of cola.

Velma's eyes widened in horror as she watched the boy fish his fangs out and wipe them on his sleeve.

'Oh no,' Yasmin said, trying to stifle a laugh. 'Looks like he's lost his bite.'

The boy put his fangs back in. 'Would you like me to show you how to be a vampire?'

Velma wrinkled her nose. 'No need, I am a vampire.'

Undeterred, the boy carried on. 'Then I'll show you how to be a better vampire. First, you need to learn how to fly.'

Velma looked puzzled. 'Fly?'

'It's easy, just flap your arms like this.'

Velma copied the boy.

'No, no, you're doing it all wrong. Maybe we'll skip the flying for now. How about turning into a bat? That's another classic vampire move.'

Yasmin panicked. The last thing she needed was Velma turning into a bat and scaring everyone. She thought quickly. 'That only works on full moons.'

The boy looked puzzled. 'That's werewolves, not vampires.'

A voice behind them interrupted, 'Did someone say werewolf?'

Velma turned around, took one look at the costume, and froze in terror.

'Hey, little vampire! What's the matter? Are you scared of the big, bad wolf?' the girl teased.

Velma whimpered and hid behind Yasmin.

The girl continued, 'Don't worry. I'll show you how to be a werewolf. It's easy. Just howl at the moon.' With that, the girl threw back her head and howled.

Velma's face turned an even whiter shade of white.

Yasmin slipped her arm through Velma's. 'Sorry, we're not interested in learning how to howl. She's a vampire, not a werewolf. And she's already pretty good at being a vampire, thank you very much.'

The girl shrugged. 'Suit yourself. But if you change your mind, just remember to howl!' she called over her shoulder as she ran off to scare some other partygoers.

Velma let out a sigh of relief. 'I don't think I like werewolves.'

'Me neither. Let's get something to eat.'

Yasmin and Velma shuffled through the partygoers towards a table draped with a black cloth and illuminated by a single black candle. On the table sat platters of grisly looking dishes, from hard-boiled eggs shaped like eyeballs to bowls of spaghetti 'guts'. Yasmin peered at a 'severed finger' that she recognised as a sausage with a sliced almond for the fingernail and ketchup for blood.

Despite Velma's enthusiasm for the spooky fare, Yasmin couldn't help but feel a little queasy. Instead, she scooped up a spoonful of dark red juice from the pumpkin-shaped bowl in the centre of the table but, before she poured it into her cup, a shoulder collided with hers and sent the cup flying. The thick scarlet liquid splattered across the walls like an explosion of blood.

Velma's eyes flared, glowing an eerie red.

Yasmin knew the signs and quickly grabbed Velma's hand, dragging her away from the table. 'Calm down, it's just beetroot juice, not blood,' she said.

Velma had only just recovered when they came face-to-face with a ghostly figure. She let out a blood-curdling scream and tried to run away, but Yasmin caught her hand.

'It's just a sheet, Velma! Like on my bed.'

But Velma wasn't having it. Despite Yasmin's attempts to reassure her, she had had enough of this party. That ghost was real, and it was coming to get her. She bolted for the nearest door and disappeared inside. 'I thought being with humans would be easier. But I don't fit in here either. I'll never belong anywhere. Not here, not back home,' she wailed.

Outside the broom closet, Yasmin tried to coax Velma back to the party by explaining that humans found it really good fun to dress up as scary things for Halloween. While Velma couldn't understand what was fun about this activity, she finally agreed it was possible the ghost was just a kid in a bedsheet and she crept out of the closet.

Having checked the ghost for evidence of a boy underneath it, Velma even relaxed enough to giggle at a coven of witches in black and purple costumes with big pointy hats and it was all going well until, out of nowhere, a zombie appeared. Velma's eyes grew to the size of saucers as she saw the decaying flesh and lifeless eyes staring back at her. She screamed. And fainted. Before Yasmin could explain about masks, leaving her wondering if perhaps it wasn't such a great idea to bring a vampire to a Halloween party after all.

Chapter 10

The Classroom Chaos

Yasmin's eyes pinged open shortly after dawn. The long awaited, and much anticipated, Bring Your Pet to School Day had finally arrived. She tugged the curtains to check the weather: it was a gloriously grey November day, exactly as she had hoped. Ideal weather for a vampire outing. No sun at all.

'Velma, wake up. You're coming to school today.' Velma half opened one eye, her face upside down. With a sigh, she let go of the ceiling, landing on her feet with a soft thud.

Yasmin shook her head. 'Velma, you have to stay as a bat! It's Bring Your Pet to School Day, and I want to bring you.'

Velma let out an exasperated sigh. 'I am many things: a night-flyer, a timeless companion, an ancient adventurer, a keeper of secrets, a midnight explorer, a vampire... but a pet? Really?'

'Think of the fun we'll have,' Yasmin begged, imagining the look on everyone's faces when she strolled in and casually said, *'Oh, this? It's just my vampire-bat.'*

Velma considered this for a moment. 'All right, for the sake of an adventure.' She turned back into a bat, buzzing around the room with a thoughtful expression. 'But...' she said as sternly as is possible when you're the size of a flying potato. 'But only if you promise to introduce me as your "extraordinary companion" and *not* your pet.'

Yasmin nodded eagerly, crossing her heart. 'Deal. The most extraordinary and exemplary companion ever.'

Over breakfast, Mum and Dad discussed the safest plan for the day. 'Perhaps a lift to school would be wise,' Dad suggested.

'Oh no, we'll be fine on the bus,' Yasmin said, picking up her school bag and settling Velma on her shoulder like a colourless parrot.

'Don't forget to stay as a bat. We don't want to scare any of the little ones,' Mum called after them.

* * *

After registration, the day started with the big pet parade. A higgledy piggledy line of furry, scaly, and feathery creatures with their proud owners wove its way across the school yard.

Yasmin headed towards the end of the line.

'I am absolutely not standing behind a rabbit,' Velma whispered in her ear, her voice filled with disgust. 'It's... it's eating a carrot!'

'Oh, Velma, it's not so bad! Just pretend you're in line at the grocery store.'

'The grocery store doesn't smell like... like... that.' Velma complained, scrunching her tiny nose and pointing a wing-tip at a nearby puppy pooping in the middle of the school yard. 'I've stared down a six-headed hydra, outflown a fire-breathing dragon, outwitted a pack of werewolves, but this... this is a whole new level of horror.'

Yasmin chuckled, patting Velma's head as they joined the parade. 'Be brave.'

'What kind of pet is that?' asked a small boy, pointing at Velma.

'Not a pet,' Velma muttered.

'She's a bat,' Yasmin explained.

The boy screwed up his eyes and squinted at Velma. 'It looks like a wrinkled rat.'

Velma rolled her eyes and stretched her wings threateningly. Yasmin shot her a warning look.

The boy stared at the bat. 'An ugly flying rat,' he declared.

That was the final straw. With a flap of her wings, Velma leapt into the air, landing next to the boy in full vampire mode. Full *angry* vampire mode. Velma glared at the boy, her red eyes blazing. 'I most definitely am NOT a rat.'

The boy screamed and the whole parade turned to look at the commotion. 'VAMPIRE!' he shouted. 'RUUUUUN!' he added, although that wasn't strictly necessary as the parade had already dissolved into chaos. Children and pets scattered everywhere, screaming and squawking, barking and meowing. Yasmin even thought she heard something moo, but she must have imagined it as who would have a pet cow. That would be ridiculous.

'You were supposed to stay as a bat,' Yasmin muttered under her breath.

'Ooops. Sorry. I could turn back? Or you could pretend not to know me. I don't want you to be ashamed of me, or to get you into trouble.'

Yasmin looked around. 'I think it's a little late for that. Just don't cause any more trouble. And I'm not ashamed of you. I could never be ashamed of you.'

'Silence!' Mr Harper said in a steely voice that sliced through the rumpus. 'Students, find your pets.

Teachers, lead your groups to their classroom. Yasmin, come here.'

Head down, Yasmin took the reluctant Velma by the hand and dragged her towards to Mr Harper.

'What do you think you were doing? Frightening the first years, that's what. Totally unacceptable behaviour. You've let yourself down, you've let the school down, and frankly I expected more from you,' Mr Harper said.

Yasmin looked at the floor and shuffled her feet. 'I'm sorry. It was an accident. Velma was supposed to stay as a bat. I know she's different, but that doesn't make her dangerous. She's my responsibility. Should I take her home?'

Mr Harper scratched his head. 'I think it might be okay for her to stay as long as we don't have any more terrifying transformations. Now, run along and join your class. You're missing history.'

Yasmin LOVED history class. They were learning about ancient Egypt and, as they snuck into the back of the room, the teacher was explaining how mummies were made. Suddenly, Velma's hand shot up. 'You definitely can't make a mummy without tacks and glue. I should know. I was there.'

The class's laughter echoed through the room while the teacher, Mrs Ortiz, blinked at Velma, her mouth opening and closing like a fish out of water. Velma grinned, flashing her vampire teeth. 'You're a v–vampire. You're imm–immortal,' she stuttered. With that, she fainted.

Yasmin elbowed Velma in the ribs.

'Ouch. What did I do?' Velma asked.

'You're scaring people again.' Yasmin rushed across the classroom to help Mrs Ortiz sit up. 'Are you okay? Can we carry on with the lesson? I promise Velma won't interrupt again.'

Next was physical education. The buzz in the school gym reached fever pitch as Miss Chopra, the sports teacher, announced the game. 'Today, we're going to practice wizard hockey, ready for the big World Book Day match!' she declared, holding aloft a battered hockey stick. 'These will be our broomsticks. You must have your broomstick with you at all times, and you can only move like this.' She held the hockey stick between her legs as if riding a hobby horse.

A murmur of excitement rippled through the class, but no one was more excited than Velma. As soon as she got her hockey stick, she was off. She zipped around the gym like a bat in a belfry, her feet never once touching the floor.

'Defence – I mean Beaters - watch out for the Bludgers,' Mrs Chopra shouted, rolling a dodgeball across the floor. 'Attack – I mean Chasers – aim for the basketball hoops. Seeker—' She looked around. 'I guess that's you, Velma, catch the golden trophy.' She whacked a gold spray-painted ping-pong ball with a bat.

'Humans really do have the most exciting games!' Velma whooped, a blur of motion as she made a spectacular dive for the golden ping-pong ball without realising she was heading straight for a towering stack of wooden benches, waiting to be set up for lunch.

'Wait! Leave it,' Miss Chopra yelled, but it was too late.

With a triumphant whoop, Velma zoomed

towards the golden ball, forgetting everything else. Unfortunately, everything else included the benches. With an almighty CRASH, Velma collided with them, sending them crashing to the ground like a game of oversized dominoes.

For a moment, there was a stunned silence in the gym, followed by a loud cheer from the class as Velma emerged from the wreckage, dazed but grinning, the golden ball triumphantly held aloft.

'Got it!' she declared, swaying slightly.

Miss Chopra rushed over. 'All right, Velma. I think it's time to visit the school nurse,' she said, guiding her away. 'Yasmin, you'd better come too. Everyone else, wait here until I get back.'

Nurse Rossi, a kindly woman with a comforting smile, finished the check-up and patted Velma's hand. 'You're fine, dear. I'm going to have a word with Miss Chopra about health and safety before the next Wizard Hockey match, but it's just a little bump on the head. Nothing a good vampire can't handle.'

Velma beamed at her. 'I told you, I'm as tough as a gargoyle knuckle.'

Nurse Rossi chuckled. 'That you are, Velma. But perhaps... well, perhaps you're a little too spirited for the rest of the school.'

'Spirited?' Velma asked, her brows furrowing in confusion. 'I'm not a ghost.'

'Not that kind of spirited. Let's just say a bit too energetic.' Nurse Rossi handed Yasmin a small slip of paper. 'This is a note for your parents. I think it would be best if you took your pet home early today, just to be safe.'

'She's not a pet, she's my friend,' Yasmin interrupted.

Velma beamed, and it's possible she blushed, although with a vampire it is hard to tell.

Chapter 11

The Bite before Christmas

Yasmin sat on her bedroom floor, surrounded by wrapping paper and Christmas gifts. She'd found something for everyone except Velma: a pair of fluffy reindeer socks for Mum, a mug adorned with a jolly Santa for Dad, and a pine-scented candle for her teacher. Now, she was on a mission to find the perfect Christmas gift for Velma. She groaned, flopping back onto her carpet. This was so much harder than she'd thought. In desperation, Yasmin messaged her friends.

Help, I don't know what to get Velma for Christmas. Any ideas?

Her phone pinged.

SOPHIE

Sunscreen?

Haha. That's not helpful.

LILY

My sister has a nice sparkly "Team Edward" T-shirt, but she is obsessed with that vampire in the "Twilight" book series.

I don't think Velma likes fictional vampires.

The chat went quiet, but Yasmin could see Chiyo was typing. She waited for her to finish; Chiyo always had good ideas. Finally, the message popped up.

CHIYO

Seriously, there's a new shop in town – Wacky Wonders Gift Shop. Their tagline is 'We specialise in unique gifts for unique people'. Maybe you could find something for Velma there?

Sounds great! Thanks, Chiyo.

Yasmin perked up. She shoved her phone in her pocket and glanced up at Velma who was lounging in bat form upside down on the ceiling, her favourite napping spot. 'Don't worry. I'll find the perfect gift for you. Just you wait and see.' She grabbed her coat and headed out the door.

* * *

Yasmin opened the door to the Wacky Wonders Gift Shop and stepped inside. A bell above her head tinkled.

'Hello. Can I help you?' asked the shop assistant, a petite woman with bright purple spiky hair and a name badge pinned to her chest identifying her as Zinnia.

'I'm looking for a gift for my pe—,' Yasmin stopped herself. 'For my friend. She's a bit... different.'

'Different, you say? Well, we specialise in unique gifts for unique people. How about this?' Zinnia suggested, holding up a certificate. 'A lifetime membership to our town's most exclusive tanning salon?'

Yasmin giggled, imagining Velma at a tanning salon. 'I'm afraid she's more of a moon-bathing type.'

'Ah, a night owl! No problem, how about this?' Zinnia continued, pointing to a dawn-simulator alarm clock. 'It's perfect for those of us who struggle to get going in the morning. Who doesn't like to wake up to a nice sunrise?'

Creatures of the night, that's who, Yasmin thought. 'She's not exactly a morning person, I'm afraid.'

'Well, you can't go wrong with a nice cookbook,' Zinnia suggested. 'This one is very popular.'

Yasmin looked at the title, *1001 Ways With Garlic*. She shuddered, remembering Velma's reaction to the garlic bread at her pizza party. 'I'm afraid she's, err, allergic to garlic. So that might not work.'

'No garlic? Got it. Well, how about this fancy selfie stick with a mirror? Perfect for capturing those memorable moments.'

Yasmin shook her head. 'I'd like that myself, but she doesn't have a reflection.'

'Aha, a camera-shy friend.' Zinnia scratched her chin thoughtfully, 'This is tricky. I know, what about a "grow your own sunflower kit"? They're proving very popular this year.'

'She's not really a sun worshipper.'

'Burns easily in the sun. Well, I guess a sunflower might not be ideal.' Zinnia looked around the shop. 'What about this wooden stick whittling kit?'

'What's whittling?' Yasmin asked.

Zinnia smiled. 'It's where you sharpen the end of the stick to make it pointy.'

'Why would you do that?'

Zinnia frowned. 'That's a good question. I've absolutely no idea, but I guess being able to make a wooden stake comes in handy if you are on a camping trip and forget your tent pegs. Or if you meet any vampires.'

'Oh...' Yasmin laughed, holding her sides. 'I think that's the least suitable gift of all!'

Zinnia joined in the laughter, oblivious to the irony. 'Well, it seems your friend really is quite unique. You know, the best gift is time. Why don't you plan to do something fun together?'

Yasmin nodded. 'That sounds perfect. I'll just get her a card now and take her to the big fireworks display on New Year's Eve. She'll love that. Thanks for the help.'

Chapter 12

The Exchange Programme

Yasmin was at her desk doing homework when she heard a flapping noise from the direction of the open window. She looked up just in time to see a tiny bat swoop into the room, barely avoiding a collision with her desk lamp.

'Whoa!' Yasmin yelped, ducking instinctively.

The bat made a quick loop around the room, then landed elegantly on the corner of her desk. Clasped in its claw was a small envelope, sealed with a crimson wax emblem. The bat dropped the envelope onto her homework, fluttered its wings once, and then, with a chittering noise that sounded suspiciously like a chuckle, disappeared off into the night.

'Bat-mail?' Yasmin said and turned her attention to the envelope that smelled faintly of garlic. There was a bat insignia embossed into the wax seal. It reminded her of the letter Harry Potter received from Hogwarts, only with fewer owls and more... bats. Because the envelope was addressed to Velma, she tucked it into the coffin lid for when she woke up.

Although she was naturally white as a sheet, Velma paled at the sight of the envelope. 'Oh no,' she said, holding it out to Yasmin. 'Please, can you read it for me? I'm too nervous. It's my exam results.'

'I didn't know you had exams,' Yasmin said, opening the letter. Inside, there was a piece of crinkly parchment. Written in blood-red ink, it read:

Dear Contessa Velma Vampira,

Congratulations! You have successfully completed your year-long exchange program and passed the 'Human Integration Exam' with a grade B+. This forms part of your

Gothic Certificate in School Education (GCSE). Your report card includes exceptional marks for 'Fang Hygiene' and 'Daytime Sleeping.' However, your scores for 'Reflection Avoidance' and 'Garlic Resistance' could use some improvement.

Yasmin turned to Velma. 'Who knew there was a 'Human Integration Exam' for vampires?'

Velma had returned to a normal shade of white. 'I can't believe I passed! I was so scared I'd fail, but you made me feel like I belong here. I couldn't have done it without you. Although it does explain why garlic bread gave me hiccups,' she confessed, and they both laughed.

'But wait, there's more,' Yasmin said, turning her attention back to the letter.

In recognition of the care and support from your host family, we are pleased to extend an invitation to your human pet—

Velma grabbed the letter, neatly crossed out the word 'pet', wrote 'F-R-I-E-N-D' in capital letters above it, then passed it back to Yasmin.

—your human FRIEND, Miss Yasmin, to spend the next academic year at the prestigious Transylvanian School of Vampire and Werewolving under our Exchange Programme as detailed in the Terms and Conditions.

Yasmin couldn't believe what she was reading. 'This can't be serious!' she gasped.

'What else does it say?' Velma asked.

Please note that all classes are nocturnal, with inset days on Full Moons. Campus rules strictly prohibit garlic and sunlight.

You can reassure your hosts that the school cafeteria offers a diverse menu ranging from Blood Type A to Blood Type O plasma pellets, with the occasional 'rabbit surprise' for our werewolf students. Exchange students are welcome to complete a 'special dietary requirements' sheet on arrival which the catering company will do their best to accommodate.

The closing date for acceptance of this

place is Friday 13th January. We look forward to hearing from you.

'You don't have to come, I know I've been more trouble than a hundred tarantulas,' Velma said.

Yasmin whooped, 'Go? Of course I want to go! We have the best fun together!' A *school for vampires* – with her best friend Velma! The idea was completely bananas... but the good kind of bananas, not the squishy ones. She could almost see the towering black castle, bat-shaped shadows swooping across the night sky, classrooms lit by flickering candles, a library stacked with dusty books that whispered when you opened them. It was weird. It was wacky. It was the adventure of a lifetime... All she had to do was persuade her parents. Which might be tricky, partly due to safety, but more because her parents thought staying up after nine o'clock was as wild as joining the circus.

Acknowledgments

I'd like to thank my neck... I mean, my next of kin for their undying support. While I haven't turned any of them into the living dead (yet), they have certainly endured their fair share of my writing process.

To Jake, Marissa, Zara and Sue, my superhuman beta readers, and Emma Mitchell, my eternal editor, I'm really 'fangful' for your keen eye and wise words. Your insights truly helped me bring this story to life... or should I say un-death?

And of course, I'd like to thank you, the reader, for being brave enough to dive into a world of extra-potent garlic bread, fang-aches, and dodgy vampire jokes. Without you, this book would be a ghost - which happens to be the theme of my next book. Hope you enjoyed it and don't forget to keep your scarf close. After all, why don't vampires have more friends? Because they are a 'pain in the neck'.

Here's to more 'fang-tastic' adventures!

Lexi

Also by Lexi Rees

The Relic Hunters Series

Eternal Seas

Wild Sky

Firestorm

Writing Skills for Children

Creative Writing Skills

Wicked Writing Skills

Mindful Mentors

Believe in Yourself (Be You)

Be More You

Other

Scavenger Art

The Fashion Fix

Horsing Around

The Book Dragon Club

Printed in Dunstable, United Kingdom

68594664R00048